THE
EMPEROR
PENGUINS

BY KAZUE MIZUMURA

THE
EMPEROR
PENGUINS

Thomas Y. Crowell Company
New York

LET'S-READ-AND-FIND-OUT SCIENCE BOOKS

Editors: *DR. ROMA GANS,* Professor Emeritus of Childhood Education, Teachers College, Columbia University
DR. FRANKLYN M. BRANLEY, Astronomer Emeritus and former Chairman of The American Museum-Hayden Planetarium

LIVING THINGS: PLANTS

Down Come the Leaves

How a Seed Grows

Mushrooms and Molds

Plants in Winter

Roots Are Food Finders

Seeds by Wind and Water

The Sunlit Sea

A Tree Is a Plant

Water Plants

Where Does Your Garden Grow?

LIVING THINGS: ANIMALS, BIRDS, FISH, INSECTS, ETC.

Animals in Winter

Bats in the Dark

Bees and Beelines

Big Tracks, Little Tracks

Birds at Night

Birds Eat and Eat and Eat

Bird Talk

The Blue Whale

Camels: Ships of the Desert

Cockroaches: Here, There, and Everywhere

*Available in Spanish

Ducks Don't Get Wet

The Emperor Penguins

Fireflies in the Night

Giraffes at Home

Green Grass and White Milk

Green Turtle Mysteries

Hummingbirds in the Garden

Hungry Sharks

It's Nesting Time

Ladybug, Ladybug, Fly Away Home

The Long-Lost Coelacanth and Other Living Fossils

My Daddy Longlegs

My Visit to the Dinosaurs

Opossum

Sandpipers

Shrimps

Spider Silk

Spring Peepers

Starfish

Twist, Wiggle, and Squirm: A Book About Earthworms

Watch Honeybees with Me

What I Like About Toads

Why Frogs Are Wet

THE HUMAN BODY

A Baby Starts to Grow

Before You Were a Baby

A Drop of Blood

Fat and Skinny

Find Out by Touching

Follow Your Nose

Hear Your Heart

How Many Teeth?

How You Talk

In the Night

Look at Your Eyes*

My Five Senses

My Hands

The Skeleton Inside You

Sleep Is for Everyone

Straight Hair, Curly Hair*

Use Your Brain

What Happens to a Hamburger

Your Skin and Mine*

And other books on AIR, WATER, AND WEATHER; THE EARTH AND ITS COMPOSITION; ASTRONOMY AND SPACE; and MATTER AND ENERGY

ISBN 0-690-26087-3
0-690-26088-1 (LB)

5   6   7   8   9   10

THE
EMPEROR
PENGUINS

LET'S
READ
AND
FIND
OUT

I went to the zoo and saw the emperor penguins. They stood on their short legs. They were black and white with a small marking of yellow on their heads.

The penguins were in a cold room at the zoo because they come from Antarctica, one of the coldest parts of the earth. They had a swimming pool because penguins spend much of their time in the water.

Penguins are birds, but they cannot fly. They don't have wings like other birds—they have flippers. Penguins use their flippers as paddles when they swim.

Penguins are good swimmers. They swim very fast.
Some can go twelve miles an hour.

Penguins have webbed feet with big claws on their
toes. They dig their claws into the ice so they
will not slip. When they walk, penguins waddle
from side to side.

They are poor runners because their legs are short.
When they are in a hurry, penguins don't run.
They slide over the ice on their white front
feathers.

Emperors are the largest of all the penguins. They stand three to four feet high. Some weigh almost one hundred pounds.

4

3

2

1

Emperors live near the South Pole, where the temperature in winter sometimes goes down to 70° below zero. Even in summer the South Pole is cold. The temperature is often 20° below zero. But penguins can live where it is very cold because they have a special way of keeping warm.

11

Stiff, short feathers cover most of the penguin's body. The feathers overlap to make a thick layer. The feathers do not get wet. They keep the penguin dry even when he swims under water. The feathers keep the penguin warm. Between his skin and the outer feathers, the penguin has another thick layer of soft feathers. The soft feathers hold in the heat of the penguin's body.

Your body makes heat. And you are always losing some of that heat through your skin. The same thing happens with a penguin, but the layers of feathers hold in the heat.

13

Penguins spend much of their time in the water.
They must swim fast to catch their food. They
eat fish and shrimp.

But penguins must be careful, or THEY will be eaten. Leopard seals and killer whales attack penguins. The penguins have to watch out for their enemies.

When nesting time comes, penguins go inland. They
go to their rookeries. These are places where
penguins lay their eggs and hatch them.
Penguins go back to the same rookeries year after
year. Sometimes there are hundreds of thousands
of penguins in a rookery.

Emperor penguins do not make nests. They stand on the ice, and the mother penguin lays one white egg. The egg weighs about one pound. It is five inches long and three inches wide.

The mother penguin passes the egg to the father by juggling the egg onto her feet. Then the father penguin draws his feet together and takes the egg onto his feet. He bends over slightly, and the soft feathers of his belly help keep the egg warm.

As soon as the mother penguin passes the egg to the father, she leaves the rookery. She goes to the sea to catch fish. She does not return to the rookery for about eight weeks.

While she is away, the father penguin guards the egg and hatches it. Male emperor penguins stand quietly together in groups while hatching the eggs. But when the snow falls and piles in deep drifts, the penguins crowd together. They lean with their beaks resting on the shoulders of the birds in front of them. By huddling together, they keep the eggs warm and keep themselves from freezing.

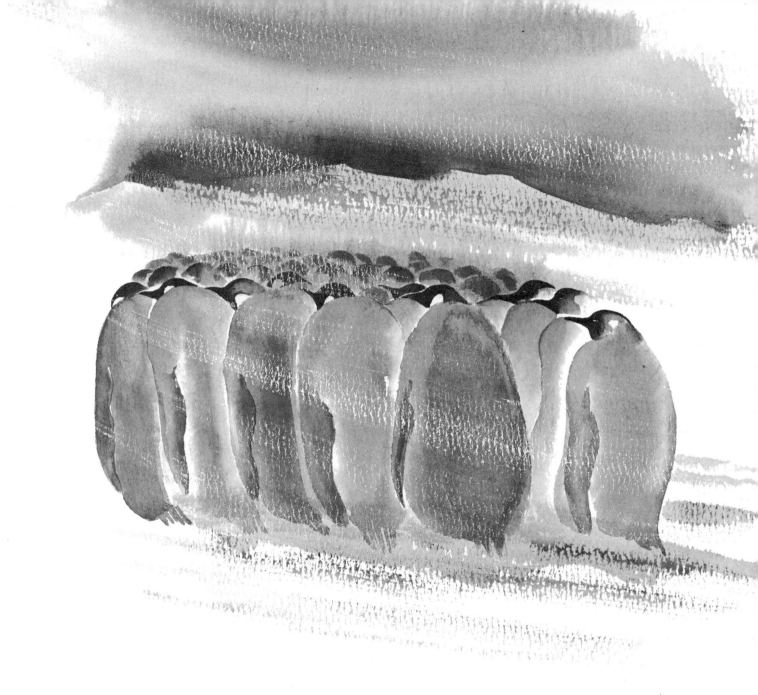

21

After about sixty-three days the egg breaks open and the baby penguin comes out. The chick has few feathers. The father keeps the chick warm in his own feathers.

The mother penguin returns about this time. She feeds her baby with the fish she caught at sea.

The father penguin has not eaten anything for nearly three months except some snow. He has lost a great deal of weight because he has been living off the fat in his body. Once the chick is hatched, the father penguin goes to the sea. Then the mother and father take turns going to the sea. They bring food back for the chick.

Penguins guard their chicks by keeping them on their large flat feet.

27

When a baby is five weeks old, the parents put the chick into a "kindergarten." Several adult penguins watch over hundreds of chicks. The parents then go on trips to bring back more fish for the growing chicks.

When a storm comes up, or when the kindergarten is attacked by an enemy, the adults make the chicks crowd together. The baby sitters form a ring around them.

When the chicks have grown old enough, all the emperor penguins go back to the sea. They swim and dive and catch their food together.

33

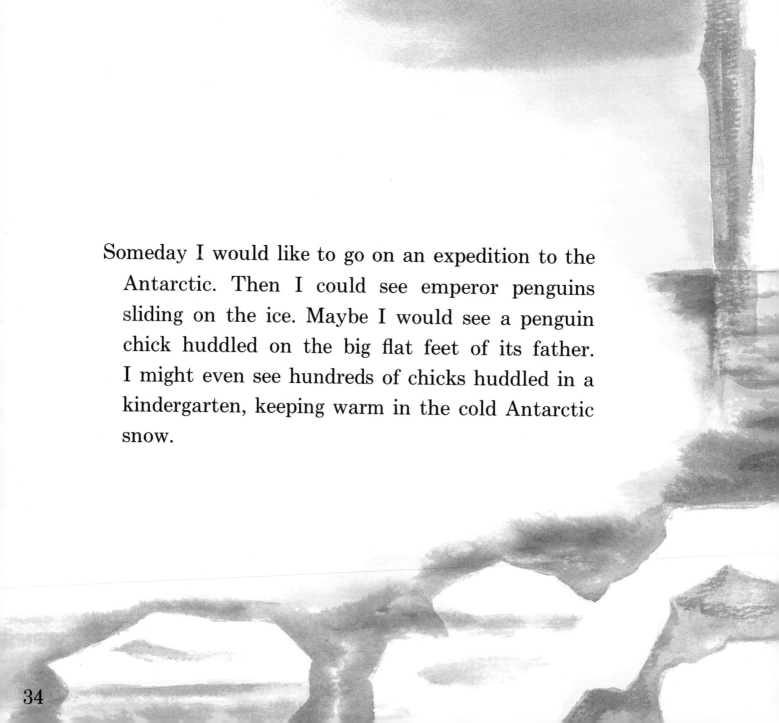

Someday I would like to go on an expedition to the Antarctic. Then I could see emperor penguins sliding on the ice. Maybe I would see a penguin chick huddled on the big flat feet of its father. I might even see hundreds of chicks huddled in a kindergarten, keeping warm in the cold Antarctic snow.

ABOUT THE AUTHOR AND THE ARTIST

Kazue Mizumura is the author and illustrator of two previous books for young readers, *I See the Winds* and *If I Were a Mother*. Her preparation for *The Emperor Penguins* included many visits to zoos and museums and libraries.

Miss Mizumura was born in Kamakura, Japan, and now lives in Stamford, Connecticut. She studied at the Women's Art Institute in Tokyo, as well as at Pratt Institute in Brooklyn, New York. Her busy life includes Japanese brush drawing and preparing advertising layouts.